SATB CHORUS AND PIANO REDUCTION

DOMINICK ARGENTO
CENOTAPH

FOR CHORUS AND ORCHESTRA

BOOSEY &HAWKES

DISTRIBUTED BY

HAL•LEONARD®
CORPORATION
7777 W. BLUEMOUND RD. P.O. BOX 13819 MILWAUKEE, WI 53213

www.boosey.com
www.halleonard.com

A **cenotaph** is a monument erected in honor of one whose remains are buried elsewhere, or whose remains cannot be recovered.

2009 Raymond W. Brock Commissioned Work
Commissioned by the American Choral Directors Association
in celebration of its fiftieth anniversary

First performed on March 5, 2009 at the
American Choral Directors Association National Convention in Oklahoma City, Oklahoma
by the American Choral Directors Association festival chorus and Oklahoma City Philharmonic Orchestra
conducted by Ann Howard Jones

CONTENTS

TEXTS

Cenotaph

I. Dedication-prelude
Orchestra only

II. Parade (Song-Books of the War)
SATB with orchestra

In fifty years, when peace outshines
Remembrance of the battle lines,
Adventurous lads will sigh and cast
Proud looks upon the plundered past.
On summer morn or winter's night,
Their hearts will kindle for the fight,
Reading a snatch of soldier-song,
Savage and jaunty, fierce and strong;
And through the angry marching rhymes
Of blind regret and haggard mirth,
They'll envy us the dazzling times
When sacrifice absolved our earth.

Some ancient man with silver locks
Will lift his weary face to say:
'War was a fiend who stopped our clocks
Although we met him grim and gay.'
And then he'll speak of Haig's last drive,
Marvelling that any came alive
Out of the shambles that men built
And smashed, to cleanse the world of guilt.
But the boys, with grin and sidelong glance,
Will think, 'Poor grandad's day is done.'
And dream of lads who fought in France
And lived in time to share the fun.

(Siegfried Sassoon)

III. Elegy (For the Fallen)
SAT with orchestra

Solemn the drums thrill; Death august and royal
Sings sorrow up into immortal spheres,
There is music in the midst of desolation
And a glory that shines upon our tears.

They went with songs to the battle, they were young,
Straight of limb, true of eye, steady and aglow.
They were staunch to the end against odds uncounted;
They fell with their faces to the foe.

They shall grow not old, as we that are left grow old:
Age shall not weary them, nor the years condemn.
At the going down of the sun and in the morning
We will remember them.

As the stars that shall be bright when we are dust,
Moving in marches upon the heavenly plain;
As the stars that are starry in the time of our darkness,
To the end, to the end they remain.

(Laurence Binyon)

IV. Chorale (Let Us Now Praise Famous Men)
SATB a cappella

Let us now praise famous men.
To them, the Lord through His majesty,
    hath apportioned great honor and glory.
Such as did rule kingdoms, men renowned
    for their power and understanding:
Leaders of the people who counseled with learning,
    eloquent and wise in their guidance:
Such as found out musical tunes to console us,
    pictures to beguile us, verses to inspire us;
All these were honored in their generations,
    and were the glory of their times;
There be of them, that have left a name behind,
    that their praises might be reported.

And some there be, which have no memorial;
    who are perished, as if they had never been;
    and are become as though they had never been born.
And these were merciful men, their glory shall not be blotted out.
Their bodies are buried in peace, but their name liveth forever.
                    (Ecclesiasticus, Ch. 44, 1–14, paraphrased)

V. Admonition (There Will Come Soft Rains–War Time)
SA with strings only

There will come soft rains and the smell of the ground,
And swallows circling with their shimmering sound;

And frogs in the pools singing at night,
And wild plum-trees in tremulous white;

Robins will wear their feathery fire
Whistling their whims on a low fence-wire;

And not one will know of the war, not one
Will care at last when it is done.

Not one would mind, neither bird nor tree,
If mankind perished utterly;

And Spring herself, when she woke at dawn,
Would scarcely know that we were gone.

                    (Sara Teasdale)

VI. Cenotaph (On Passing the New Menin Gate)
SATB with orchestra

Who will remember, passing through this Gate,
The unheroic Dead who fed the guns?
Who shall absolve the foulness of their fate,–
Those doomed, conscripted, unvictorious ones?
Crudely renewed, the Salient holds its own.
Paid are its dim defenders by this pomp;
Paid, with a pile of peace-complacent stone,
The armies who endured that sullen swamp.

Here was the world's worst wound. And here with pride
'Their name liveth for ever' the Gateway claims.
Was ever an immolation so belied
As these intolerably nameless names?
Well might the Dead who struggled in the slime
Rise and deride this sepulchre of crime.

                    (Siegfried Sassoon)

VII. Tattoo (The Last Post*)
Wordless SATB a cappella with solo bugle

* "The Last Post" is played every evening by buglers at the war
memorial in Belgium known as the Menin Gate, commemorating
the British Empire dead at the Battle of Ypres during WWI.

INSTRUMENTATION

Orchestra:
Flute 1, 2
Oboe 1, 2
B♭ Clarinet 1, 2
Bassoon 1, 2

F Horn 1, 2, 3, 4
C Trumpet 1, 2, 3
Trombone
Tuba

Timpani
Percussion 1, 2

Harp

Strings

duration:
c. 25 minutes

Performance materials are available from the Boosey & Hawkes Rental Library.

Cenotaph

I. Dedication-prelude

II. Parade (Song-Books of the War)

Siegfried Sassoon

The voices enter as indicated, improvising spoken remarks about an approaching parade with impatience, ever-growing excitement and ultimately cheers – their volume coordinated with the orchestra's crescendo.

Lyrics in the vocal staves:

plun - dered past. On sum - mer morn or win - ter's night, Their hearts will kin - dle

for the fight, Read-ing a snatch of sol - dier - song,_____ Sav-age and jaun - ty,_____

11 **Stesso tempo ma gioioso** ♩ = *100*

Stesso tempo ma gioioso ♩ = *100*

12 **Largamente** ♩= *92 ca.*

14

Poco meno mosso ♩ = 88

S: en-vy us the daz-zling times _____ When sac-ri-fice ab -

A: en-vy us the daz-zling times _____ When sac-ri-fice ab -

T: en-vy us the daz-zling times _____ When sac-ri-fice ab -

B: en-vy us the daz-zling times _____ When sac-ri-fice ab -

Poco meno mosso ♩ = 88

13 **Tempo del comincio** ♩ = 106

ff decrescendo coll'orchestra

S: solved our earth. _____

A: solved our earth. _____

Voices improvising remarks and cheers as before.

T: solved our earth. _____

B: solved our earth. _____

Tempo del comincio ♩ = 106

decrescendo

16 Stesso tempo ma maestoso assai

boys, with grin and side-long glance, Will think, 'Poor gran-dad's day is done.' __ And dream of

boys, with grin and side-long glance, Will think, 'Poor gran-dad's day is done.' __ And dream of

boys, with grin and side-long glance, Will think, 'Poor gran-dad's day is done.' __ And dream of

boys, with grin and side-long glance, Will think, 'Poor gran-dad's day is done.' __ And dream of

lads who fought in France __ And lived in time to share the fun. __

lads who fought in France __ And lived in time to share the fun. __

lads who fought in France __ And lived in time to share the fun. __

lads who fought in France __ And lived in time to share the fun. __

III. Elegy (For the Fallen)

Laurence Binyon

18

spheres, _____ There is mu - sic _____ in _____ the midst of des - o -

spheres, _____ There is mu - sic _____ in _____ the midst of des - o -

spheres, _____ ...mu - sic _____ in _____ the midst of des - o -

la - tion _____ And a glo - ry that shines up - on our

la - tion _____ And a glo - ry that shines up - on our

la - tion _____ And a glo - ry that shines up - on our

IV. Chorale (Let Us Now Praise Famous Men)

Ecclesiasticus,
Ch. 44, 1–14

V. Admonition (There Will Come Soft Rains–War Time)

Sara Teasdale

Cantabile e dolcissimo ♩ = 52

Soprano: There will come soft rains and the smell of the ground, And swal-lows cir-cling with their shim-mer-ing sound; And frogs in the pools sing-ing at night, And

Alto: There will come soft rains and the smell of the ground, And swal-lows cir-cling with their shim-mer-ing sound, the swal-lows cir-cling; And frogs in the pools sing-ing at night, And

VI. Cenotaph (On Passing the New Menin Gate)

Siegfried Sassoon

The final four measures are repeated several times, gradually fading into silence, the various sections of the chorus should arrive at inaudibility at different times, i.e., not simultaneously.

VII. Tattoo (The Last Post*)

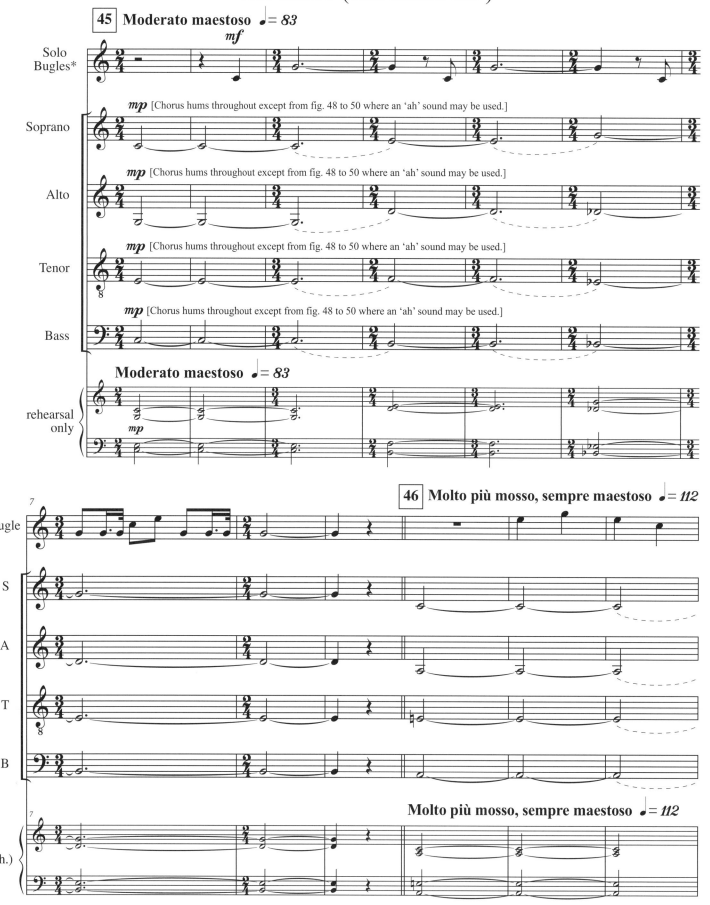

* "The Last Post" is played every evening by buglers—usually a group of three or more—at the war memorial in Belgium known as the Menin Gate, commemorating the British Empire dead at the Battle of Ypres during WWI.